When My Pen Bleeds

Also by Rick Mapson

Seeing Clearly – A View from Heaven
Coffin Train
The Box
The Little Tree Who Whispered Help
The Caterpillar Who Dreamt She Could Fly

When My Pen Bleeds

Poetry and Shorts by

Rick Mapson

Almond Blossom Community, LLC
Miller, MO 65707

AlmondBlossomCommunity.com

Almond Blossom Community, LLC
Miller, MO 65707

Copyright © 2024 by Rick Mapson
All rights reserved.
No part of this book may be reproduced in any form or by any electronic or mechanical means including information storage and retrieval systems, without permission in writing from the publisher, except as provided by United States of America Copyright law. The only exception is by a reviewer, who may quote short excerpts in a review.

ISBN- 978-1-948630-09-2

Printed in the United States of America

09 08 07 06 05 04 03 02 01

First Printing: September 12, 2024

Table of Contents

When My Pen Bleeds 7
A Tear Fell 8
Are You Out There? 9
Clarity, Thought, and Purpose * 10
Depth 11
Dust Merchant 12
Failed 13
Fool's Gate 14
Gold 15
Good sayings 16
I Didn't Know 17
Inverted 18
Lonely is the Glass 19
May They Rest in Peace 20
My End 21
On the other side of the Glass 22
Pondering 23
Quiet and Still 24
Reflections 25
The Fear Brokers 26
The open scar 27
The Watcher 28
Today I feel really small 29
Today I was Alive 30
Today 31
When 32
Words 33
I Cried Today 34

The Label Maker	35
I'm Sorry	36
A Sweet Moment	37
Inside	38
Change	39
Cows on Bikes	40
Love Stinks	41
Nobody Knows	42
O to the Blooming Flower	43
Sonnet #1	44
When the Light Won't Change	45
Raven Remix (Evermore)	46
Waves	51
Flying	52
I Don't Know	54
Invention Incorporated	56
The Trip	60
Just a Thought	61
Just Stop It	62
Letting Go	63
Oh, What Will Grow	64
Quiet	65
Why	66

When My Pen Bleeds

© Rick Mapson 10/6/2014

When a thought comes into my head
My emotions not far behind
Silly funny or dreary dread
It is then I find

My Father in Heaven
Is waiting to see
What I will create
What will come to be

Creation stirring
Mind weaving
As nothing becomes something
When my pen bleeds

A Tear Fell
© Rick Mapson 12/2012

A tear is puddling in my eye.

A tear is puddling, do you want to know why.

I got to tell how you're doing and it made me proud.

Sorrow and sadness no longer show on your face.

Butterflies and moonbeams have taken their place.

Things that all little girls should be allowed to dream.

You did good.

Are You Out There?

© Rick Mapson 11/2011

Unseen minions
    waiting waiting cold numb
Afraid of being seen
    afraid as being seen as dumb

Once you were a doer
    now most things left undone
Your heart no longer beats
    It's no longer fun

Being part
    not being whole
Has left you empty
    with yearning in your soul

Are you out there in this darkness
    darkness that we share
Let us come together
    and together we will care

Clarity, Thought, and Purpose *
© Rick Mapson 6/2010

If I produce reports in print and Excel but have not purpose. I am only a beautiful PowerPoint document headed for the shredder.

If I have the power of the internet and can understand Facebook and Twitter, and if I have clarity that can search massive databases, but have not purpose, I am nothing. If I give all my downloads to management and surrender my unwanted PowerPoint to the shredder, but have not purpose, I gain nothing.

Purpose is like rain, that becomes a stream, that become a pond, that becomes a river, that becomes a sea, that becomes a cloud. Purpose is life to weary bones and peace to the mind. It does not delight in deadlines and time but rejoices in thought and clarity. It does not mind unperfected ideas but rejoices in creativity and discovery.

Purpose never lacks energy. But where there is uncreative work, it will cease. Where there are limits, they will be breached. Where there is worthlessness, it will pass away. For now, we discover what is known to us, but when creativity comes, we will become like our father. While I am alive, I will talk and think like someone who will die, but when I die, I will talk and think like someone who is alive. I will have clarity beyond any thought I have ever known, and true adventure will be my purpose. The greatest adventure of all, getting to know the creator of all things, my Father.

And now these three remain: Clarity, Thought, and Purpose. But the greatest of these is Purpose.

* Winner of Best Poem - 2018 Colorado Christian Writers Conference

Depth

© Rick Mapson 06/2013

Hard Shallow Puddle
    catches a glimmer.

Deep Waters
    embrace and treasure it.

Gold
    you pass to the next Generation.

Dust Merchant
© Rick Mapson 7/2013

I am the Dust Merchant.
That's not how I started,
    or what I thought I'd become.
I worked hard creating and collecting.

But then one day I found something real,
    something that would last.
It was then I knew everything I had was dust,
    that someday would just blow away in the wind.

The harder I tried the create or collect things,
    that were real.
The more the things of dust tried to consume,
    all my time,
        all my resources.
That is how I became the Dust Merchant.
Storing up
    things
        that won't last.
Dust Merchant,
    it's not who I am,
        just what I've become.

Failed

Rick Mapson © 2011

Called to set up a meeting
    no answer, Failed.
Sent an email to set up a meeting
    no response, Failed.

Paying bills
    no money left, Failed.
Disappointment
    in you, Failed.

Can't pay mortgage,
    lost home, Failed.
Found another home,
    mice, Failed.

Fool's Gate

© Rick Mapson 5/2011

Enter all who seek knowledge.

Enter to become wise.

Join those who can open the floodgate of data
          to the delight of the masses.

Live where procedures rule and paradigm shifts
          astound the keepers of academia.

Take part in manufacturing data to support needed truth
          that will transform society.

Be induced to tweak logic and skew science to produce needed resul[ts]
          for the good of civilization.

Ascend to the depths of an ideologue… if you are deemed worthy.

Humbled and self-satisfied within your own certitudes.

Able to look down at all passersby.

—

—

—

          Oblivious of the Gate you built that

              now holds you in.

Gold

© Rick Mapson 06/2013

There once was a young husband.
There once was a young wife.

Together they searched for treasure.
They search hard and one day they found it!
A bright shiny nugget.

They were so happy until they were told they could no longer mine there and had to leave their shiny nugget behind.

They were so sad that they stopped mining. Then one day a longing became a desire and blossomed into hope.

They started their search again. This time they found a Mother Lode. More precious than gold, that would bless their family and the world.

Dare to love again.
Your Mother Lode awaits and can be found in Him.

Good sayings
© Rick Mapson 4/2010

The Day we run out of
    Options is the day we
        Stop growing.

Making a Dollar is better Than,
      saving a Dollar

Saving a Dollar may save Me but
        Making a Dollar may save Us.

A Penny saved,
        is Not a Penny earned.

Fear and Hoarding are Brothers,
      who serve the same master.

Today was Tomorrow,
      Just Yesterday.

Time stops for no man,
        But will slow down when threatened.

I Didn't Know
© Rick Mapson 7/2014

I didn't know I was a slave until you broke my leg…

so, I couldn't run.

I didn't know you hurt me till you looked away.

I didn't know I talked too much until you fell asleep.

I didn't know I didn't matter until there was no room for me.

I didn't know you cared until I saw the puddle in your eye.

I didn't know I was alone until I didn't want to be.

I didn't know.

Inverted
© Rick Mapson 8/2011

Fragmented pieces

Pieces of string

Jumbled knots of everything

Knowing

Not knowing

And knowing not

Can't help healing the pain I got

Pit in my gut

Not for food or drink

From doing

Not doing

And doing not

Up has become down

And down is not

What I thought would do

Did not

So I sit here not doing

And not doing

And not doing a lot

Lonely is the Glass
© Rick Mapson 4/2011

Lonely is the glass
    That peers out through the night
        keeping out the cold.

Lonely is the glass
    That allows the warmth of the sun to pass through
        without holding the rays for itself.

Lonely is the glass
    That holds water for others to drink
        not ever taking a sip.

Lonely is the glass
    That becomes invisible
        so others can see.

I long for the beach.

May They Rest in Peace
© Rick Mapson 1/2012

A hand not touching the gravestone,
                        just hovering above.

A heart that holds the tongue from speaking
            while it takes its time
                    shedding tears.

Feet that are heavy and don't want to move,
       that somehow transport you away,
             to that new familiar foreign place
                  where life tries to bring you
                      back from the dead.

My End
© Rick Mapson 10/2010

Unknowingly I drink of the rejection of the hurried as I try to point to the abyss. I can smell its all-consuming hunger, ready to devour. I too continue down the ever-increasing ascent hopeful that I am wrong this time confident that I am not.

Once again, I cry out a warning after they have covered their ears. Maybe this time I will just follow them in. Then I won't have to live this nightmare over because I too will be at my end.

Must we always travel the path well-trod? What is in us that causes us to trust others more than we trust ourselves? Discoveries and New Worlds beckon us, but we can't trust ourselves because we know we are human.

This we fail to see "in the others" as the excitement of this new relationship will surely save us from the old. We are put at ease with their experience as they take us where they want to go.

So, we quietly go to our end not wanting to take the responsibility that would require us to make a difference with our lives.

On the other side of the Glass
© Rick Mapson 2009

Life is lonely on the other side of the glass.
I try not to linger on the other side of the pane.
Longing to see them and missing what I thought we had.
Hoping they don't see me. Wishing they would.
Not sure if they ever did…

Once long ago, inside, with them was I,
or at least in the building where I could hear and smell the food.

A few times they asked me to sit with them a few minutes
before they left. Alone in their presence, oh what bliss.
I just noticed someone else spy through the glass.
I think they were looking for memories just as I
Seeing their sadness caught in the pane.

I don't know where it came from, but my voice called out
their name.

I saw the tear they tried to hide, as they looked down in shame.

We both stared at the cracks in the pavement as we went
on our way,
our backs to each other fading away.

So, if you see me glancing through the glass at you.
Please just ignore me because we both know what is true.
I must remain lonely because that is what I am meant to do.

Pondering
© Rick Mapson 6/2012

I have pondered many thoughts,
    in my head

Knowing a fool, I could be.

    If my brilliance I let them see

        So, I kept my tongue silent instead.

Quiet and Still
© Rick Mapson 08/2013

Being in a place Quiet and Still

So far removed
      so distant
            faded
                  silent
Waiting
      hearing
            starting to see
                  the unseen

Glimmering start
      of a thought I can't grasp

Waiting waiting
      for it to come nearer

To come
      fully in view

Just to marvel
      in its simplistic
            complexity

To be known once
      by me

and never
      once more

Reflections
© Rick Mapson 1/2011

Is it true

    all I can see is reflection.

  Light bouncing

    into my eye.

  Giving me

    beauty.

  Making me

    sigh.

The Fear Brokers
© Rick Mapson 2/2010

Scare

Stimulated   with   Money (Grants, Bailouts, Stimulus)
Controlled   by   Privileged (Politician, scientist, ministers, educators)
Advanced   for   Greed (Power, Oppression, Control)
Received   in   Ignorance (Nearsighted, shortsighted, limited)
Established   through Fear (need, trust, blindness, deception)

Are you a Social Terrorist?

What can you be wrong about?

What can't you be wrong about?

Is it okay for someone to have another opinion?

Do you allow those in your group or vocation to SCARE others?

Can your words stand on their own without you yelling them?

Are you an EAP (Easily Agitated Person, sheep) allowing yourself to be SCAREd?

Science has always been about discovery of our world. Taking the best information we have to find out how things work or to help determine where we need to be. New or more current information is the life blood of science which helps remove or change old ideas no matter how good they seemed. Saying, "ALL the information is in" should send shivers down the back of anyone that cares about truth.

Remember: "I AM THE GREAT and POWERFUL OZ, don't look at the man behind the curtain!"

[27]
The open scar
© Rick Mapson July 2012

The scar is open and will not close

Time goes by and memories fade

Everything but what's in the scar

That face

    That smell

        That sound

The haunting effects of what should not have been

    but were

        silent stay around

Days linger

    Nights entomb

Staring at the scar

    No longer even asking why

Maybe someone

    Someday may break my stare

By asking me just one more time

    To share

I'll look away like I always do

    but this time I'll let you in.

The Watcher
© Rick Mapson April 2002

I am the watcher. It was not a position I have chosen but given. I am required to watch as the waves of despair and sadness swallow the one I love. When I try to do something, anything by throwing out a lifeline you are driven out repelled by my attempt driven deeper into the waves.

My heart breaks as I sit, my intentions bound in chains. My pain surrounds me as silent laughter reminds me that I am alone in a world that requires that I suffer in silence. I wander through the hall of our memories; times that brought joy, unable to ignore the sadness lapping at my feet. I must push away the sorrow and be strong. I wish they knew that in reality I am a weak reed afraid of snapping while being pulled out to sea.

As long as I sit and watch, you come closer to shore. Sometimes your friends bring you close enough that I can hear your laughter. In the past, thinking the tide had changed; I have rushed out with joy to hold you in my arms. Just to find you stiff and driven back into the deep. Now I just watch through bittersweet tears. Happy that joy is back in your life sad that I am not.

Lord, you are my refuge and strength. To you and you alone can I cry. You are my comfort helping me make it through another day.

Then one day to my surprise.

You came over and sat by my side.

I looked at you and you started to sing.

The fog has lifted it's now become spring.

Today I feel really small
by Rick Mapson © 5/2011

Today I feel really small

Not very anything not very anything at all

Something I should have planned for I didn't see

Someone I should have been but wasn't able to be

I'm sorry that I couldn't doesn't make it right

Knowing that I didn't draws me into the night

Your tender hand your loving smile

Please, I don't deserve it, could you stay for awhile

I so long to belong

Knowing you will stay, will help me become strong

Today I was Alive
© Rick Mapson 10/29012

Today I was Alive
    but I did not Live.
I did the things
    I always did.

I worked I ate
    I drove through town.
With little ups
    and little downs.

No longer dreaming
    dreams I dreamt.
No future no time
    to be spent

So if you like me are Alive
    but do not live.
Try helping a dreamer
    try to give.

Today

© Rick Mapson July 2010

Today
    Someone made a difference in my life.

They
    Eased my pain and relived my strife.

Cared
    Enough to help me make it thru.

For me
    That Good Samaritan
                Was You.

When
© Rick Mapson 1/2011

When your time is gone and you're ready to go.
When the song has ended and you're standing alone on the floor.
When you keep hearing your cell phone ring, but no one has called.
When you're stuck between tears and headed for the door.

Remember someday, someplace, somehow

Everyone will know the truth

Of who you really were

Not what you've

Become

.

Words

© Rick Mapson 11/2011

Words once cherished
    now fallen on the floor.
Words that were welcomed
    now kindly swept out the door.

Words once honored
    no longer given the time of day.
Words once longed for
    now wished they would go away.

Words no longer asked for
    still, come to my heart
Words crying out
    wanting to be a part.

Words no longer written
    on paper damp with tears.
        Words only whispered to Heaven
        with the broken
            and the feared.

I Cried Today
© Rick Mapson 11/2013

I thought of a story and started to write.

The day that was day turned into night.

Life flooded in leaving my writing out.

I so long to write as the days pass away.

Sad at their going with nothing to say.

Only tears to mark their passing.

As their stories fade.

The Label Maker

© Rick Mapson 5/2012

There once was a label maker who loved to make labels.
He would look you up and down and say "Hum"
Sometimes he would ask a few questions and say "Uhhuh"
Then he would give you a Label and that is who you were.
No matter what.

You could try to give yourself another label but it wouldn't work.
Many people would be given the same label.
The Label Maker meant well.
He wanted everyone with the same label to stick together.
That way they could belong and help each other.

Everything sounded good and should have gone well.
In the beginning, it did, but then it started to go wrong.
The problem was in his Labels.
He made them so quickly by how you looked or what you did.

He didn't take the time to find out who you were.
That would take too long and what if he was wrong?
So he stood by his label because they were always right.
Everyone knew they were so most sat by silently as things got worse.

He never created labels of right or wrong.
He never created labels for good or bad.
If someone with the same Label did something bad.
You had to call it good, so you wouldn't look bad.

Anyone caught saying something bad about someone who wore the
same label was given the Label of Traitor or Fool.
Truth, Justice, and Goodness were held captive for the sake of Unity
that kept everyone divided and so it goes, and so it goes.

Do you hide behind your Label?
Does it allow you to be less than you could be?
If so, Tear it off quickly and join those who are free.

I'm Sorry
© Rick Mapson 9/2012

I'm Sorry I didn't see you.
I don't think I really looked.
The glimpse I took caused me to turn, away.
Allowing you to fade in the mist.

I'm sorry I didn't even give you a smile.
Underestimating its worth.
If somehow you ever read this.
We who don't always show it, really do care.

A Sweet Moment

© Rick Mapson 5/2012

Today the Sun came out and made me happy.

Not that it Made Me happy, but I allowed it to touch me.

It didn't literally touch me, but its rays did.

Anyway, for a moment it made me happy.

A simple happy in the middle of chaos

Like the penguin you swear waved to you from an iceberg

Causing you to forget for a sweet moment,

that you are standing on the deck of the Titanic.

Inside
© Rick Mapson 4/2014

I showed some of myself today.
A piece of my heart.
I gave away.

You didn't laugh.
You didn't ignore.
You walked right in and opened the door.

Looking inside.
You were careful to tread.
Walking among the living and the dead.

Feeling sad for the loss.
Happy for the gain.
Able to know my gladness and my pain.

Seeing the hidden.
The still and the proud.

Thanks!

Change

© Rick Mapson 4/2019

Just when we think things won't change
Snow begins to melt as longer days appear
Spring awakes from its sleepy slumber
With its bold array of colors

The rains have subsided heat has taken hold
Just when we think things won't change
Fruit begins to appear where buds once were
Long green grass in fields turn to gold

Heat of day turns to the cool of the night
Welcome harvest days of plenty and thanks
Just when we think things won't change
Red Gold Yellow turns Brown crunching under feet

Wind blows to chill the bone and leaves to rattle
The once dying now sleep covered with snow
A silent stillness with stars all aglow
Just when we think things won't change

Cows on Bikes
© Rick Mapson 4/2019

Cows on bikes
        How can this be
Strange and bizarre as this seems
        The only one staring is me

Even the mother
        With five kids in tow
Don't even notice
        Don't seem to know

I just stood there
        Frozen in place
As a bovine and her calf
        Join in the race

Then came a threesome
        All sharing one bike
With signs on their backs
        Sam, Charlie, and Ike

Still, no one stirred
        Or looked all about
Even when one when by
        Eating a trout

Then I noticed my glasses
        Were as dirty as could be
So I huffed on each glass
        And wiped on my tee

I looked for the cows
        That I could no longer see
Life was back to normal
        I guess that's how it should be

Love Stinks

© Rick Mapson 4/2019

Love floats
> Through the wheat fields
>> Into my arm

Love is
> There at the end
>> Of every day

Love doesn't care
> When I'm complaining
>> I get kisses all the same

Love…

> Mom Love stinks

> Honey that's not nice

I really mean it, mom
Love rolled in the cow's manure again
Love Stinks!

Nobody Knows
© Rick Mapson 4/2019

Nobody knows my smile
My mask I let them see
A world I now live in
A world that doesn't know me…

Nobody knows my heart
The one you gave cause to sing
That now walks with the hollow
No happiness to bring…

Nobody knows I dance
How I would spin and twirl with you
Fall asleep in the meadow
Awaking with the dew…

Nobody knows I see you
In the shadows of the day
Sometimes I forget and talk to you
Like you had never gone away…

Nobody knows I'm dying
Life goes on without a care
I hear the plans they're making
Knowing I won't be there…

Nobody know the peace I have
That my maker cares so for me
Helping me on this journey
As stillness cradles me…

Nobody knows I'm floating
No more pain and sorrow to know
There you are you're smiling
Like I remembered from so far below…

O to the Blooming Flower
© Rick Mapson 11/2019

O to the blooming Flower
With your stem raised on high
Your scent fills the valley
For all who breathe its air

Your petals draw
The dancers who
Shuffle with delight
On your swaying floor

The wind as your partner
Tossing you to and fro
Together creating music
That only silence knows

Today I sweep through that valley
That has saved a ticket for me
O to the blooming flower
Who longs to dance with me

Sonnet #1

© Rick Mapson 10/2019

Appalled I forgo the train
Repent then forget until tomorrow
Strolling I unleash refrain
Infecting my core to the marrow

Critiquing prose as music die
Past orange window crows await
Walk past balloons where corpus lie
Success peaks past Phantom gate

Underneath life blood flow
Feeding those who despair
Death gives way as flowers grow
Patching bridges needing repair

As evening sets and whispers still
Morning wakes against my will

When the Light Won't Change
© Rick Mapson 10/2019

That's how they became the Brady
 A three-hour tour

People let me tell you 'bout My Best
 A three-hour tour

And make me happy and make Me
 A three-hour tour

Up from the ground came A bubblin
 A three-hour tour

Monday Tuesday happy
 A three-hour tour

Come and knock on our door We've been waiting for
 A three-hour tour

Come aboard. We're expecting
 A three-hour tour

Keep Manhattan, just give me the country
 A three-hour tour

Our whole universe was in a hot dense
 A three-hour tour
  A three-hour tour

[46]

Raven Remix (Evermore)
© Rick Mapson 11/2019

ONCE NODDED, NAPPING, TAPPING,
RAPPING, RAPPING
MY DOOR, MY DOOR
AND NOTHING MORE.

AH, BLEAK DECEMBER
WROUGHT UP THE MORROW
FROM MY BOOKS OF SORROW
LOST ANGEL EVERMORE.

SAD RUST ME
ME FELT NOW
BEAT MY HEART
MY DOOR, MY DOOR

MY SOUL FACT
YOU RAPPING, TAPPING, TAPPING
MY DOOR, OPEN DOOR
DARK NOT MORE

DEEP DARK DREAM
DREAM TO DREAM SILENCE BROKEN
TOKEN, SPOKEN WHISPERED
WORD WORD NOT MORE

MY SOUL BURNING,
LOUD THEREAT EXPLORE
THIS MY LORE NOTHING MORE

SHUTTER FLIRT FLUTTER,
STATELY SAINTLY STOPPED
HE WITH LORD OR LADY
MY DOOR, MY DOOR
NOTHING MORE

EBONY BIRD BE MY GRAVE
BE SHORN AND NO GRIM SHORE
ME ON NIGHT'S SHORE!
EVERMORE.

VELLED THIS FOWL
ITS ANSWER BEING
HIS DOOR HIS DOOR,
EVERMORE.

LONELY SOUL UTTERED FLUTTERED
MUTTERED HER FRIENDS
OWN THE MORROW
EVERMORE.

STARTLED BROKEN REP SPOKEN,
DOUBT IT UTTERS FROM SOME MASTER
DISASTER FOLLOW FOLLOW FASTER
BURDEN BORE BURDEN BORE
EVERMORE.

STILL IN MY FANCY
SMILING I LIED AND BUST DOOR;
VELVET SINKING, MYSELF THINKING
GRIM, GHASTLY, GAUNT, MEANT
EVERMORE.

GAGED THE FIERY EYES
BURN MY BOSOM'S CORE
DIVINING, RECLINING ON VELVET LINING
GLOATED O'ER, VELVET-VIOLET O'ER,
AH, EVERMORE!

METH AIR GREW DENSER
FROM UNSEEN CENSER
FOOT TINKLED ON THE FLOOR.
I CRIED, OH QUAFF THIS KIND AND FORGET
EVERMORE.

THING OF EVIL STILL
TOSS HERE ASHORE,
DAUNTED, ENCHANTED, HAUNTED
I IMPLORE, I IMPLORE!
HE EVERMORE.

EVIL HEAVEN THAT BENDS US
WE ADORE THIS SOUL WITH SORROW
WITH THE ASP A ANGELS CLASP
QUOTH HE EVERMORE.

WORD I SHRIEKED
NIGHT'S SHORE!
LEAVE AS TOKEN SPOKEN! UNBROKEN!
MY DOOR! MY DOOR!
QUOTH HE EVERMORE.

HE FLITTING, SITTING, STILL SITTING
MY DOOR; ALL SEEMING DREAMING, STREAMING
HIS SHADOW THE FLOOR; THE FLOOR
SHALL BE LIFTED—EVERMORE!

The Second Coming

© Rick Mapson 11/2019

Twisting and twisting the knots unwind
The hunting dog returns to no master;
Planes fall from the sky, reality slips:
Sheer revolution is the lot of those remaining:
The zombies are loosed, searching endlessly:
The pretense of goodness lies naked:
The good no longer have restraint, while evil
Are eager to fulfill fear.

Without a doubt, we are in Revelations:
Without a doubt the Second Coming is.
The second coming! The words still echo in my ear
When transported by the spirit
Horror vex my vision: somewhere by the sand of the sea
A beast of a lion with the head of a man,
Black eyes stare hollowed by the sun.
Slowly muscles flex, at their gait.
While shadows lurk half gull half raven.
As darkness covers light again: I now know
That millennium of deafness deep into the night
Woke to nightmares by an empty cradle,
And what evil, our lust bid come at last,
Crouches toward the Holy to be born?

Waves

© Rick Mapson 10/2018

I see you lying there so peaceful and still.
A kind of satisfaction on your face.
The toil of life all through.
No more pain to suffer, no more running this race.

Then another wave hits me.
I'll miss you. I miss you.
I know you've already said goodbye.
But words are still dry in my mouth.

The wave passes…
Your rhythmic breathing lets me drift away.
To memories of better days. Hunting, fishing, quiet still together
Interrupted only by the shot of a gun or tug on the line.

I drift away to Emigrant Basin spillway.
Watching field mice run about,
A buck enters the clearing as you raise your rifle.
I feel another wave building somewhere inside.
Instead of a shot ringing out the monitor goes off.

Dazed, I open my eyes to see the nurse rush into the room.
Turning the monitor off she stands there frozen.
She mouths the word "sorry" all sound is sucked from the room.
The wave hits again as I look at him.

This time there is no breath to comfort me.
Crowded by loved ones, we all feel alone.
I can feel the wave pass,
Soon I will be able to breathe.

      * * *

Days have become weeks and weeks have become years.
I have grown to welcome the waves.
Pausing to let them wash over me.
Bringing whatever they will.

Some are small and I hardly notice.
Some drive me to my knees.
Thankful for the memory of you.

Flying
© Rick Mapson 4/2016

Two small leaves
Chasing each other in the wind
Traveling round and round
Who will win

The little one's ahead
Now the big one takes its place
Oh what fun
My what a race

Closing my eyes
Cool wind blowing in my face
Memories flood in
My mind starts to race

To be caught up high
Oh what bliss
Recalling your beauty
And your tender kiss

[53]

I Don't Know
© Rick Mapson 8/2016

What would I do
When things I believed
Were found untrue
What would I do

I'm sure I would check
 And Check
  And Check
   Again

What will I do
When what I believed was wrong
Would I ignore truth
Or sing that new song

If I bury what I learned
And try to get along
No one would know
That I drowned out that song

But if that melody
Continues, playing in my head
Consuming my bitterness
Destroying my dread

[55]

Would I wake up
Singing that song
Singing it all morning
Singing it all day long

Others would know
But what do I care
Smiling with the truth
I want to share

Sure I am different
The trapped scoff at me
But peace is my friend
I'm truly free

Invention Incorporated
© Rick Mapson 11/2016

"My paper I dropped it right here."

"So."

"What do you mean so, I need it Ben."

"Was it good, Isaac? Did it have gravitas?"

"What! Franklin, look behind the stove."

"Nice stove Isaac, I think I see it behind the pipe in the corner."

Ben grabbed the paper tearing it on one side as he waved it above his head. "Is it Newton worthy, man? Gravitas does it have gravitas. Does it matter?"

"It is matter and I dropped it but being paper the wind (when you opened the door) the wind blew it to the corner. Of course it has Gravitas! I like that word it reminds me of grave or pudding."

Isaac, "What does grave have to do with pudding?"

"Gravity!"

"What?"

"Ben, grave and pudding are just words I like."

"You are insane, Isaac. Gravity what is gravity?"

"My new word."

"Your new word."

"Yes, my new word I just invented."

"You can't do that!"

"What?"

"Just pick a new word out of thin air like you're picking an apple off a tree."

"An apple off a tree! Ben, you are a genius."

"Isaac, you have been cooped up too long."

"Franklin, wind would not affect an apple dropping from a tree. Paper works but the calculations are too hard. I would have to discover math that most people would hate."

"Not if you called it something snappy like Calculations-R-Us."

"Calculus, I could call it Calculus."

"Do I get credit for your new math?"

"No."

"How about giving me your kite, Isaac?"

"Sure, why not Ben. You can become a regular Mary Poppins."

"Isaac, wind could affect a falling apple."

"Not on a calm day."

"Of course, not on a calm day."

"Ben, it affects everything, not just apples."

"Wind?"

"No, not wind Ben, gravity."

"Everything! How about light, Isaac. Does it affect light."

"I do not think so but maybe even light."

How about a smile.

"No, Ben not a smile, not a look, not a glance. But without a belt it will pull down your pants."

"How do you know?"

"It was math of course."

"Great. Because of math I have to wear a belt."

"There you have it Ben. I have just invented Gravity the theory of falling things."

"Can I blame you if I drop a box of apples on my foot?"

"No."

"But, it could be proved that your gravity forced the box on my foot."

"My gravity. I just discovered it. It would be seen as an act of God. Check your insurance acts of God are not covered."

"You said you invented it!"

"No I did not."

"You sure?"

"Of course I'm sure. After we eat we must go out to the orchard."

"I am hungry, where is the bakers son little John Montague? You did order the bread."

"Of course Ben, even I know you must have bread with figs and rice."

"Why do you want to go to the orchard Isaac?"

"So you can knock an apple out of the tree on my head?"

"So, you can sue God?"

"I already told you. You cannot sue God. I need a good story."

"A good story?"

"Yes Ben, I need a good story for my invention, I mean discovery."

"A paper dropping to the floor does not have the drama you seek, Mr. Newton".

"Not really, but your aim must be good. I need the apple story to be real. John is here."

Ben opened the door just as John started to knock on the door.

"Mr. Franklin I do not care for your opening the door before I knock."

"Sorry, I asked Ben to open it. Please excuse the pranking pleasure of an old man."

"Oh, I did not see you Mr. Newton."

"Join us lad." Isaac said to Ben's frown.

John smiled, "Thank you sir."

"Ben, please serve us a few plates. When we are done I would like to send a meal with John here to poor Richard. That ok with you son?"

"Yes, sir."

"The reason he is poor is all he does it talk and he keeps all our plates."

"Ben he does come up with some zingers, but the plates is a problem."

"Isaac, I have a solution. I will cut two pieces of bread and put the rice and figs between them. Then young John here can wrap it up in paper. The bread will keep the paper from getting wet."

"Ben that is the craziest thing I have ever heard."

"Just common sense, Mr. Newton."

The Trip

© Rick Mapson 4/2016

Martha, we need your help. The city is too crowded and with the war not safe anymore. You need to encourage them to get on the train. They will be going to the countryside. It is beautiful this time of year. It's for their own good. We know the trains won't be very comfortable, but we didn't have much time to get things ready. The war you know.

Martha weaved her way through the crowded train station telling anyone who would listen.

"The city is too crowded and not safe anymore."

"You get to go to the countryside; it's very beautiful this time of year."

"I know the trains are crowded but we don't have much time."

Many of the people knew Martha. That she was good and honest. So they boarded the train with little fuss.

As the last group was boarding Martha started to cry. "I will so miss my friends and they are going to such a wonderful place."

"This train is not for you", came the reply.

Martha cried harder. "Why can't I go? Am I not good enough to go to this beautiful place?"

"Are you sure?"

Martha composed herself. "Yes, very sure."

"Make room in that last car."

Martha and her friends were so happy as she stepped into the car.

The Train was ready, and the transportation order was given to the conductor who quickly opened it. Go straight through. No Stops. Destination: Auschwitz.

Just a Thought

© Rick Mapson 9/2021

Words cast out
        On the waters
With no one to hear
        Sink beneath the waves

I'm screaming inside
        Can you hear me
My sorrow carries me down
        I'm silent now

Still waiting

They say
        Still waters run deep
Then why
        Am I still in the kiddie pool

Sometimes I hate words
        They're sweet on my tongue
But become bitter
        With nowhere to go

Still waiting
        Not being read

Still here
Yep
Touch any lives
        Nope

I'm just a thought
        No one searches to hear

Just Stop It
© Rick Mapson 03/2015

Just Stop It
    when you're going the wrong way.

Just Stop It
    when you have nothing good to say.

Just Stop It
    Before you make someone cry

Just Stop It
    even if you don't know why.

Letting Go
© Rick Mapson 9/15/2015

I'm watching the wave
        saying good-bye
To the pain I've been holding
        making me cry

Seeing it drift
        out of sight out of view
In its place
        my heart is being renewed

I hear laughter
        that has been there all along
But pain and bitterness
        had drowned out that beautiful song

I know I held on far too long
        unable to forgive
            to somehow move on

You didn't know
        and could probably care less
I drank the poison you gave
        that turned grace into bitterness

I know something will happen
        trying to turn spark to flame
That anger that feeling
        when I hear your name

Lord, may I see your smile
        you gave me when you said to let it go
You showed me how sad they look
        with their meanness in tow

Lord help me to be kind
        and spread the love you share
To the lost and the lonely
        and even those who don't care

Oh, What Will Grow
© Rick Mapson 6/2016

When Darkness becomes light
    and cold becomes warm
When dawn awakens
    after the storm

A new day will awaken
    that will swallow the past
New seeds will be planted
    a new die will be cast

Sure there will be struggles
    but you won't be alone
Working hard will be good
    for something of your own

You might not notice
    not right away
The gradual changes
    will seem to come in a day

You'll sit and ponder
    reflect on the past
On the day
    you let hatred go

Quiet

© Rick Mapson 5/2016

Here in the Moon's glow
    Shining bright
In the silent stillness
    Of night

Your gentle memories
    Caress my face
With your beauty
    Full of grace

Time be still
    Let me remember more
Don't be quick
    To close my mind's door

Times together
    Flow on by
Set adrift
    With your smile

Why

Rick Mapson © 10/2014

The sun that warmed me, bringing me to life.

Now scorches me from the inside out.

I fall into the pit of the forgotten.

Covered by darkness, hardened and alone.

Dreams long dead in silence, I lie.

The ache and dread grow inside.

Outside sealed against good and evil.

Time passes as I debate my death.

Can't see, hear, or feel. I must be dead.

I drift off as more time passes.

Still, here, I awake to nothing.

Debate and drift off again.

The shell cracks and all that is dead pushes out into the darkness.

Out in the darkness searching for the memory of what was light.

Pushing mountains aside for that first glimpse.

The warmth pushes me on.

Then it happens.

I am bathed in light and warmth.

Rain comes and is no longer a terror.

I drink in its goodness.

I grow larger each day.

Somehow, I know someday I will have seeds of my own.

They will be happy for a while.

Then they will wither and die.

Sadness and loneliness will come.

After death, they will understand why.

www.ingramcontent.com/pod-product-compliance
Lightning Source LLC
Chambersburg PA
CBHW060541080526
44586CB00012B/816